Delicious Whoopie Pies Recipes You Can't Resist!

The Grand Cookbook for Whoopie Pies!

Table of Contents

Introduction

You are welcome to this part of the recipe book, and you're here because you chose this recipe book to help you learn about more whoopie pies Recipes.

You're in the best place to learn about Whoopie pies as this recipe book has a lot of Whoopie pies recipes that you'd look to recreate over and over!

With this recipe book and the whoopie pies recipes that it contains, there is absolutely no dull time! You are sure going to have a lot of fun!

Thank you once again for buying this recipe book.

See you on the next page!!!

Chapter 1 – Whoopie Pies for Everyone: Chocolate, Vanilla, and Fruity Whoopie-Pie Recipes

Lemon and Blueberry Whoopie Pies

Serving: 16 whoopie pies

Prep Time: 25 to 30 minutes

Bake Time: 12 minutes

Total Time: 37 to 42 minutes

Ingredient List:

- 1 cup unsalted butter, softened
- 2 large eggs, room temperature

- 1 teaspoon of baking powder
- ½ teaspoon baking soda
- 1 pint fresh blueberries
- 2 teaspoons vanilla
- 1 cup sugar
- 2 ½ cups purpose, all-flour
- 1 teaspoon salt
- ½ cup milk
- Lemon filling, see Chapter 4

Instructions:

a. Preheat oven to 350 F. Line the bottom of 2 baking sheets with a parchment paper. Set aside.

b. Combine all the dry ingredients together in a bowl. Set aside.

c. Cream the sugar and butter together until smooth. Add in the eggs, followed by the vanilla. Mix until fully incorporated.

d. Combine the dry mixture with the wet mixture until fully combined. Fold in the blueberries.

e. Drop the batter onto the prepared baking sheets by 1 ½ tablespoonfuls, making sure to keep them about 2-inches apart.

f. Bake in the oven for 12 minutes. Once done, remove from the oven and let them cool completely on a wire rack.

g. Assemble the whoopie pies by spreading the Lemon Filling (recipe found in Chapter 4), between two of the cookies. Store the treats in a fridge for up to 7 days.

Brownie Whoopie Pies

Serving: 24 whoopie pies

Prep Time: 20 minutes

Bake Time: 8 to 10 minutes

Total Time: 28 to 30 minutes

Whoopie Pie Ingredient List:

- ½ cup unsalted butter, melted
- 1 large egg, room temperature
- 1 brownie mix

Filling Ingredient List:

- 2 tablespoons whipping cream
- ½ cup unsalted butter, softened
- ½ cup marshmallow cream
- 1 teaspoon vanilla
- 2 cups powdered sugar
- ½ cup cocoa powder, unsweetened

Instructions:

a. Preheat oven to 350-degrees F. Line the bottom of 2 baking sheets with parchment paper. Set aside.

b. Combine the butter, brownie mix, and egg. Roll the dough into 1-inch balls and place on the prepared baking sheet. Bake in the oven for 8 to 10 minutes.

c. Remove the baking sheet from the oven and let the cookies cool on a wire rack.

d. Make the filling by beating the marshmallow cream, butter, whipping cream, and vanilla together until fluffy. Beat in the powdered sugar and cocoa powder.

e. Assemble the whoopie pies by spreading the icing between two of the cookies. Store the treats in a fridge for up to 7 days.

Oreo Whoopie Pies

Serving: 14 to 16 whoopie pies

Prep Time: 30 minutes

Bake Time: 7 to 8 minutes

Total Time: 37 to 38 minutes

Whoopie Pie Ingredient List:

- ½ cup water, warm
- 2 cups flour, all-purpose

- ½ cup cocoa, unsweetened

- 1 large egg, room temperature

- ½ cup buttermilk

- ¼ teaspoon salt

- 1 teaspoon vanilla extract

- 1 teaspoon baking soda

- ½ cup unsalted butter, softened

- 1 cup sugar

Filling Ingredient List:

- ½ cup unsalted butter, softened

- 4 cups powdered sugar, sifted

- ½ cup shortening

- 15 Oreo sandwich cookies, crushed

- 6 ½ tablespoons heavy cream

- 1 ½ teaspoons vanilla extract

Instructions:

a. Preheat the oven to 400-degrees F. Line the bottom of 2 baking sheets with a parchment paper. Set aside.

b. Cream the sugar and butter together until fluffy and light. Add the vanilla and salt, followed by the egg. Set aside.

c. In a second bowl, sift the flour, cocoa, and baking soda together. Gradually combine this mixture with the butter mixture, alternating the mixture with the buttermilk and water.

d. Drop the mixture onto the prepared baking sheet by the teaspoonful and bake in the oven for 7 to 8 minutes. Once done, remove from oven and let cool.

e. Make the filling by whipping the shortening and butter together until smooth. Add in the powdered sugar and vanilla until everything is well incorporated. Mix in the heavy cream until smooth and creamy. Fold in the crushed Oreo cookies.

f. Assemble the whoopie pies by spreading the icing between two of the cookies. Store the treats in a fridge for up to 7 days.

Fruity-Pebbles Whoopie Pies

Serving: 16 whoopie pies

Prep Time: 25 minutes

Bake Time: 8 to 9 minutes

Total Time: 33 to 34 minutes

Whoopie Pies Ingredient List:

- ½ cup shortening, butter-flavored
- ½ teaspoon salt
- 1 ½ teaspoons baking soda
- ½ cup buttermilk
- ½ cup water, hot
- 1 large egg, room temperature
- 1 cup Fruity Pebbles cereal, crushed lightly
- 1 cup sugar
- 2 ½ cups flour, all-purpose
- 2 teaspoons vanilla
- Marshmallow Buttercream filling, see Chapter 4

Instructions:

a. Preheat oven to 400-degrees F. Line the bottom of 2 baking sheets with parchment paper. Set aside.

b. Cream the sugar and shortening together until the mixture is fluffy and light. Whisk in the egg, followed by the water, buttermilk, and vanilla until fully incorporated. Set aside.

c. In a separate bowl, sift the flour, salt, and baking soda together. Gradually add this mixture to the sugar mixture from Step 2 until well incorporated. Add the crushed Fruity Pebbles and gently fold into the batter.

d. Drop the batter by 1 ½ tablespoonfuls onto the prepared baking sheet. Bake in the oven for about 8 to 9 minutes. Remove the whoopie pies from the oven and let them cool.

e. Assemble the whoopie pies by spreading Marshmallow Buttercream filling (recipe found in Chapter 4) between two of the cookie pies. Roll the sides of the whoopie pies in crushed Fruity Pebbles until they stick to the filling.

f. Store the treats in a fridge for up to 7 days.

Cookie-Dough Whoopie Pies

Serving: 12 whoopie pies

Prep Time: 20 minutes

Bake Time: 6 to 7 minutes

Total Time: 26 to 27 minutes

Whoopie Pie Ingredient List:

- 1 cup milk
- ½ cup cocoa powder, unsweetened
- 2 tablespoons vanilla
- ½ teaspoon salt
- 1 large egg
- 1 cup granulated sugar
- 1 ½ teaspoons baking soda
- 2 cups flour, all-purpose
- ½ teaspoon baking powder
- ½ cup shortening
- Chocolate-chip filling, see Chapter 4

Instructions:

a. Preheat oven to 450-degrees F. Line the bottom of 2 baking sheets with parchment paper. Set aside.

b. Combine the cocoa powder, flour, baking powder, baking soda, and salt together. Mix in the shortening and sugar.

c. In a separate bowl, combine the milk, egg, and vanilla. Combine this mixture with the flour mixture from Step 2.

d. Drop the batter onto the prepared baking sheet by the tablespoonful and bake in the oven for 6 to 7 minutes. Remove the cookies and let them cool.

e. Assemble the whoopie pies by spreading chocolate-chip filling, recipe found in Chapter 4, between two of the cookies. Store the treats in a fridge for up to 7 days.

Chunky-Monkey Whoopie Pies with Banana Filling

Serving: 12 whoopie pies

Prep Time: 10 minutes

Bake Time: 8 to 10 minutes

Total Time: 18 to 20 minutes

Whoopie Pie Ingredient List:

- ½ cup water
- 3 large eggs, room temperature
- 1 box chocolate cake mix
- ½ cup vegetable oil

Filling Ingredient List:

- ¼ cup walnuts, chopped
- ¼ cup mini chocolate chips
- 16 ounces heavy cream
- ½ cup powdered sugar, sifted
- 5 ounces pudding mix, banana cream

Instructions:

a. Preheat oven to 400-degrees F. Line the bottom of 2 baking sheets with parchment paper. Set aside.

b. Mix the cake mix, water, eggs, and oil together until well combined. Drop the batter onto the prepared baking sheets in heaped tablespoons. Bake in the oven for 8 to 10 minutes. Once done, transfer the cookies to a wire rack to cool.

c. Make the filling by whipping the heavy cream for several minutes until peaks begin to form. Add the pudding mix and powdered sugar and continue to whip until well combined.

d. Assemble the whoopie pies by spreading the icing between two of the cookies. Roll the sides of the whoopie pies in a mixture of the chocolate chips and walnuts, until they stick to the filling. Store the treats in a fridge for up to 7 days.

Chocolate Whoopie Pies with Nutella Filling

Serving: 14 whoopie pies

Prep Time: 20 minutes + 30 minutes to chill

Bake Time: 8 to 10 minutes

Total Time: 58 to 60 minutes

Whoopie Pie Ingredient List:

- ¼ cup sugar, granulated
- ¾ cup buttermilk
- 1 ¾ cups all-purpose flour

- ½ cup unsalted butter, softened

- ½ cup cocoa powder, unsweetened

- ¾ cup brown sugar, packed

- 1 teaspoon baking soda

- 1 teaspoon vanilla

- 1 large egg, room temperature

Filling Ingredient List:

- ½ cup unsalted butter, softened

- ¾ cup Nutella hazelnut spread

- 2 ½ tablespoons milk

- 1 teaspoon vanilla

- 4 cups powdered sugar

Instructions:

a. Preheat the oven to 350-degrees F. Line the bottom of 2 baking sheets with parchment paper. Set aside.

b. Cream the butter and sugars together until light and fluffy. Mix in the vanilla and the egg. Stir in the flour, cocoa, and baking soda until well mixed. Fold in the buttermilk. Cover the mixture and place in the freezer for about 30 minutes.

a. Preheat the oven to 350-degrees F. Line the bottom of 2 baking sheets with parchment paper. Set aside.

b. Cream the butter and sugars together until light and fluffy. Mix in the vanilla and the egg. Stir in the flour, cocoa, and baking soda until well mixed. Fold in the buttermilk. Cover the mixture and place in the freezer for about 30 minutes.

c. Roll heaped teaspoonfuls of the chilled mixture into balls and place on the prepared baking sheet. Bake in the oven for 8 to 10 minutes. Once done, remove from the oven and let them cool.

d. Create the filling by beating the butter until smooth. Add the sugar and mix until light and fluffy. Stir in the vanilla, followed by the Nutella and the milk.

e. Assemble the whoopie pies by spreading the icing between two of the cookies. Store the treats in a fridge for up to 7 days.

Chapter 2 – Get into the Spirit: Seasonal Whoopie Pie Recipes

Spiced-Pumpkin Whoopie Pies with Cinnamon, Maple, and Browned Butter Filling

Serving: 36 whoopie pies

Prep Time: 30 minutes

Bake Time: 12 to 14 minutes

Total Time: 42 to 44 minutes

Whoopie Pie Ingredient List:

- 1 teaspoon salt

- ¾ cup vegetable oil

- 1/8 teaspoon nutmeg

- 2 large eggs, room temperature

- 1 teaspoon ginger

- 1 teaspoon baking soda

- 1 teaspoon baking powder

- 3 cups flour, all-purpose

- 1 ½ teaspoons vanilla

- ¼ cup butter, melted

- ¼ teaspoon cloves

- 2 teaspoons cinnamon

- 2 ¾ cups canned pumpkin

- 2 cups brown sugar, packed

Filling Ingredient List:

- 1/8 teaspoon cloves

- 5 tablespoons unsalted butter, softened

- 1 tablespoon pure maple syrup

- 1/8 teaspoon salt

- 3 cups powdered sugar, sifted

- 4 ounces cream cheese, softened

Instructions:

a. Preheat oven to 350-degrees F. Line the bottom of 2 baking sheets with a parchment paper. Set aside.

b. Whisk the flour, salt, baking powder, cloves, baking soda, cinnamon, ginger, and nutmeg together in a bowl.

c. In a second bowl, cream the butter, brown sugar, and oil together until smooth. Mix in the eggs, one at a time, followed by the vanilla and pumpkin. Continue mixing for about a minute.

d. Gradually stir the flour mixture in the pumpkin mixture until just combined.

e. Drop the dough by the tablespoonfuls onto the prepared baking sheet, keeping each mound of dough about 2-inches apart.

f. Bake in the oven for 12 to 14 minutes. Once done, remove from the oven and let them cool on a wire rack.

g. Make the icing by melting the butter in a saucepan over medium heat. While stirring constantly, continue to cook the butter until it turns a golden brown color. Remove from the heat and let it cool for about 10 minutes.

h. Cream the cream cheese with the cooled butter from Step 7 until fluffy and light. Mix in the maple syrup, salt, nutmeg, cloves, and cinnamon until combined. Gradually mix in the powdered sugar until smooth.

i. Assemble the whoopie pies by spreading the icing between two of the cookies. Store the treats in a fridge for up to 7 days.

Cotton-Candy Whoopie Pies

Serving: 24 whoopie pies

Prep Time: 40 minutes

Bake Time: 9 minutes

Total Time: 49 minutes

Ingredient List:

- 1 large egg, room temperature

- 1 can Duncan Hines Frosting Starter

- 1 packet Duncan Hines Cotton-Candy Flavor Mix

- ½ cup unsalted butter, melted

- 1 box Confetti cake mix

Instructions:

a. Preheat the oven to 350-degrees F. Line a baking sheet with parchment paper. Set aside.

b. Combine the cake mix, egg, and butter until well combined. Cover the mixture and let it chill in the fridge for 25 to 30 minutes.

c. Remove the mixture from the fridge. Roll the dough into 1-inch balls. Place the dough balls on the prepared baking sheet from Step 1.

d. Bake the dough balls in the oven for 9 minutes. Once set in the middle, remove from oven and let them cool completely on a wire rack before continuing.

e. Make the filling by stirring the flavor packet into the frosting until fully incorporated.

f. Assemble the whoopie pies by spreading the filling between two of the cookies.

Gingerbread Whoopie Pies with Cream Cheese Filling

Serving: 24 whoopie pies

Prep Time: 1 + hours to chill + 30 to 35 minutes

Bake Time: 11 to 13 minutes

Total Time: 1 hour and 41 minutes to 1 hour and 48 minutes

Whoopie Pie Ingredient List:

- ½ teaspoon salt

- ¼ cup molasses

- ¾ teaspoon baking soda

- 2 teaspoons cinnamon

- 2 cups flour, all-purpose

- Powdered sugar, dusting

- ¾ cup light brown sugar, packed

- 8 tablespoons unsalted butter, melted

- 1 large egg, room temperature

- ¼ cup buttermilk

- 3 tablespoons ginger (crystallized), chopped finely

- ½ teaspoon nutmeg

- 1 teaspoon vanilla

- ¼ teaspoon cloves

- ½ teaspoon ginger

Filling Ingredient List:

- ½ teaspoon vanilla

- 1/8 teaspoon salt

- 1 ½ cups powdered sugar, sifted

- 6 tablespoons unsalted butter, softened

- 6 ounces cream cheese, softened

Instructions:

a. Combine the flour, ginger, salt, cloves, nutmeg, baking soda, and cinnamon together in a bowl. In a separate bowl, cream the butter and sugar together, followed by the crystallized ginger and molasses. Add the egg, vanilla, and buttermilk until well combined. Gradually mix in the flour mixture. Cover the bowl and chill in the fridge for 1 or more hours.

b. Preheat oven to 350-degrees F. Line the bottom of 2 baking sheets with parchment paper. Set aside.

c. Roll tablespoons of the chilled dough into balls. Place on the prepared baking sheet, making sure to keep each dough ball about 2 inches apart.

d. Bake in the preheated oven for 11 to 13 minutes. Once done, remove from the oven and let them cool.

e. Make the filling by beating the butter and powdered sugar together until light and fluffy. Add the softened cream cheese and beat until well combined. Mix in the salt and the vanilla.

f. Assemble the whoopie pies by spreading the icing between two of the cookies. Dust the whoopie pies liberally with powdered sugar. Store the treats in a fridge for up to 7 days.

Apple Whoopie Pies

Serving: 18 whoopie pies

Prep Time: 10 to 15 minutes

Bake Time: 10 to 12 minutes

Total Time: 20 to 27 minutes

Ingredient List:

- 1 teaspoon apple-pie spice
- ¼ cup milk

- ¼ teaspoon salt

- 2 ½ cups flour, all-purpose

- 1 large egg, room temperature

- 1 Granny Smith Apple, skinned and grated

- ½ cup unsalted butter, softened

- 1 teaspoon baking soda

- ¼ cup applesauce

- 1 ¼ cups brown sugar, packed

- Cinnamon and Cream Cheese filling, see Chapter 4

Instructions:

a. Preheat oven to 350 F. Line the bottom of 2 baking sheets with a parchment paper. Set aside.

b. Cream the butter and brown sugar together. Once light and fluffy, add in the apple-pie spice, salt, and baking soda.

c. Add the egg and mix until fully incorporated. Do the same for the milk and applesauce. Gradually stir in the flour and then fold in the grated apples.

d. Drop the batter onto the prepared baking sheet by the tablespoonful and bake in the oven for 10 to 12 minutes.

e. Take the whoopie pies out of the oven and let them cool on a wire rack before continuing.

f. Assemble the whoopie pies by spreading the Cinnamon and Cream Cheese Filling (recipe found in Chapter 4) between two of the cookies.

Chapter 3 – Everything Else: Other Whoopie-Pie Recipes

Lavender Whoopie Pies

Serving: 12 to 20 whoopie pies

Prep Time: 15 minutes

Bake Time: 6 to 8 minutes

Total Time: 21 to 23 minutes

Whoopie Pie Ingredient List:

- 1 cup sugar
- ¼ cup vegetable oil
- 1 teaspoon vanilla
- 4 teaspoon lavender flowers, dried
- ½ teaspoon salt
- 2 ¼ cup flour, all-purpose
- ¼ cup whole milk
- ¼ teaspoon baking soda
- Purple food coloring
- 2 large eggs, room temperature
- ½ cup Greek yogurt, plain
- ¼ cup unsalted butter, softened
- 1 ¼ teaspoons baking powder
- Vanilla Bean filling, see Chapter 4

Instructions:

a. Preheat the oven to 350-degrees F. Line the bottom of baking sheets with parchment paper. Set aside.

b. Process the lavender, yogurt, milk, and vanilla together in a food processor for about a minute.

Strain the pieces of lavender from the mixture, making sure to rub the lavender pieces with a spatula to release their natural oils. Set the mixture aside.

c. Whisk the baking powder, salt, baking soda, and flour together. In a second bowl, cream the butter, sugar, and oil until smooth and fluffy. Add the eggs, one at a time, followed by a few drops of the food coloring until you achieve the desired tint.

d. Gradually stir the milk mixture into the butter mixture until well combined. Slowly mix in the flour mixture until just combined.

e. Drop the dough onto the prepared baking sheet by the heaped teaspoonful, making sure to keep each mound of dough a couple of inches apart.

f. Bake in the oven for 6 to 8 minutes, or until the middle of the whoopie pie is done. Remove from the oven and let them cool.

g. Assemble the whoopie pies by spreading the Vanilla Bean filling (recipe found in Chapter 4) between two of the cookies. Store the treats in a fridge for up to 7 days.

Root-Beer-Float Whoopie Pies

Serving: 12 to 14 whoopie pies

Prep Time: 15 minutes

Bake Time: 10 minutes

Total Time: 25 minutes

Whoopie Pie Ingredient List:

- 3 cups all-purpose flour
- ¾ cup buttermilk

- ¼ cup shortening, room temperature

- 1 large egg, room temperature

- ¾ cup dark brown sugar, packed

- ½ cup unsalted butter, softened

- ½ cup milk

- ½ cup granulated sugar

- 1 teaspoon baking soda

- 2 ½ teaspoons root-beer extract

- 1 teaspoon salt

- ½ teaspoon vanilla

Filling Ingredient List:

- ½ cup butter

- 3 cups powdered sugar, sifted

- 1 to 2 teaspoons milk

- ½ cup shortening

- 2 teaspoons vanilla extract

Instructions:

a. Preheat oven to 375 F. Line the bottom of 2 baking sheets with a parchment paper. Set aside.

b. Cream the butter, sugars, salt, and shortening together until smooth. Mix in the remaining ingredients for the whoopie pies until well combined.

c. Spoon about 2 tablespoons of the batter onto the prepared baking sheet, making sure to leave 2-inches between each mound of batter.

d. Bake in the oven for 10 minutes or until the middle of your whoopie pies are set. Remove the baking sheet from the oven and let them cool on a wire rack.

e. While the whoopie pies are cooling, make the filling by whisking all the ingredients together until smooth.

f. Assemble the whoopie pies by spreading the icing between two of the cookies. Store the treats in a fridge for up to 7 days.

Red-Velvet Whoopie Pies

Serving: 12 whoopie pies

Prep Time: 25 minutes

Bake Time: 10 to 12 minutes

Total Time: 35 to 37 minutes

Whoopie Pie Ingredient List:

- 2 teaspoons vanilla
- 2 cups flour, all-purpose
- 3 tablespoons cocoa powder, unsweetened
- ½ teaspoon salt
- 1 large egg, at room temperature
- ½ cup unsalted butter, softened
- 2/3 cup buttermilk
- Red food coloring
- 1 cup light brown sugar, packed
- 1 teaspoon baking soda
- Cream Cheese filling, see Chapter 4

Instructions:

a. Preheat oven to 350-degrees F. Line the bottom of 2 baking sheets with parchment paper. Set aside.

b. Sift the baking soda, flour, salt, and cocoa powder together into a mixing bowl. Set aside.

c. In a second mixing bowl, cream the butter until smooth. Mix in the brown sugar until well combined and fluffy. Mix in the egg, followed by the buttermilk and vanilla.

d. Gradually mix the dry ingredients from Step 2 into the wet ingredient from Step 3 until just incorporated.

e. Add enough food coloring into the mixture so that the dough is a deep red color.

f. Spoon mounds (about 1 ½ tablespoons for each mound) of dough onto the prepared baking sheet. Make sure to keep each mound about 3-inches apart.

g. Bake the dough in the preheated oven for 10 to 12 minutes or until the middle of each mound is set. Once done, remove from the oven and let cool on a wire rack.

h. Assemble the whoopie pies by spreading the Cream Cheese Filling (recipe found in Chapter 4) between two of the cookies. Store the treats in a fridge for up to 7 days.

Mini Carrot-Cake Whoopie Pies

Serving: 10 whoopie pies

Prep Time: 25 minutes

Bake Time: 8 to 10 minutes

Total Time: 33 to 35 minutes

Ingredient List:

- 2 tablespoons vegetable oil
- ½ tablespoon nutmeg

- 1 teaspoon vanilla
- 1 cup grated carrots
- 1 large egg, room temperature
- 1 cup flour, all-purpose
- ¼ teaspoon baking soda
- 1 tablespoon cinnamon
- ¼ cup unsalted butter, melted
- ½ teaspoon salt
- 2 teaspoons orange rind, grated
- 2/3 cup light brown sugar, packed

Instructions:

a. Preheat oven to 350 F. Prepare a baking sheet by lining it with a parchment paper. Set aside.

b. Mix the flour, salt, sugar, nutmeg, cinnamon, and baking soda together. Set aside.

c. In a separate bowl, mix the melted butter, vanilla, vegetable oil, egg, and orange peel together. Gradually combine the wet mixture into the dry mixture until well combined.

d. Fold in the grated carrots until well incorporated. Roll the dough into small 1-inch balls. Place the dough balls onto the prepared baking sheet, making sure to keep each dough ball about 2-inches apart.

e. Bake in the preheated oven for 8 to 10 minutes. Once done, remove from the oven and let them cool on a wire rack.

f. While the pies are cooling, make the filling by creaming the butter and cream cheese together, followed by the vanilla. Cover the filling and let it chill in the fridge for about 20 minutes.

g. Assemble the whoopie pies by spreading the icing between two of the cookies. Store the treats in a fridge for up to 7 days.

Mini Snickerdoodle Whoopie Pies

Serving: 20 to 24 whoopie pies

Prep Time: 30 minutes

Bake Time: 10 to 13 minutes

Total Time: 40 to 43 minutes

Whoopie Pie Ingredient List:

- 3 tablespoons cinnamon-sugar mixture + extra for garnish
- 2 tablespoons cake enhancer

- 1 teaspoon baking powder

- 2 ½ cups all-purpose flour

- 1 teaspoon salt

- 1 teaspoon baking soda

- 1 teaspoon vanilla

- 1 large egg, room temperature

- 2/3 cups cinnamon baking chips, mini

- 1 teaspoon cinnamon

- 1 cup whole milk

- ½ cup shortening

- 1 cup brown sugar, packed

Filling Ingredient List:

- ¾ cup unsalted butter, softened

- 3 tablespoons meringue powder

- 2 cups powdered sugar, sifted

- ¼ teaspoon vanilla-butternut flavoring

- 1/3 cup water

Instructions:

a. Preheat oven to 350-degrees F. Line the bottom of 2 baking sheets with parchment paper. Set aside.

b. Beat the sugar, shortening, vanilla, and egg together until well mixed. Set aside.

c. Combine all the dry ingredients and then gradually add them to the sugar mixture from Step 2. Fold in the cinnamon chips.

d. Drop the cookie dough by the teaspoonful onto the prepared baking sheet. Make sure to keep the dough balls are an inch or so apart.

e. Bake in the oven for 10 to 13 minutes. Once they are firm to touch, remove the baking sheet from the oven. Let them cool completely.

f. Make the filling by beating the water and meringue powder together until the mixture becomes foamy. Add the sugar and vanilla-butternut flavoring, and beat until well combined. Beat in the butter until the mixture is smooth and fluffy.

g. Assemble the whoopie pies by spreading the icing between two of the cookies. Store the treats in a fridge for up to 7 days.

Butterfinger Whoopie Pies

Serving: 10 to 12 whoopie pies

Prep Time: 15 to 20 minutes

Bake Time: 11 to 12 minutes

Total Time: 26 to 32 minutes

Whoopie Pie Ingredient List:

- ½ cup sour cream

- ½ cup unsalted butter, softened

- 1 box Butterfingers cookie baking mix

- 2 large eggs, room temperature

Peanut Butter and Cream Cheese Filling Ingredient List:

- 2 cups sifted powdered sugar

- 8 ounces cream cheese, softened

- 1 teaspoon vanilla

- ½ cup peanut butter, creamy

Instructions:

a. Preheat oven to 350-degrees F. Prepare 2 baking sheets by lining them with parchment paper. Set aside.

b. In a mixing bowl, cream the butter until smooth. Beat in the eggs, one at a time, and the sour cream until well mixed. Gradually stir in the cookie mix until just combined.

c. Spoon mounds (about 1 tablespoon for each mound) of dough onto the prepared baking sheet. Make sure to keep each mound about 1 to 2-inches apart.

d. Bake the dough in the preheated oven for 11 to 12 minutes or until the middle of each mound is set. Once done, remove from the oven and let them cool on a wire rack.

e. While the pies are cooling, make the icing by creaming the cream cheese and peanut butter together until smooth and creamy. Mix in the vanilla, followed by the sifted powdered sugar.

f. Assemble the whoopie pies by spreading the filling between two of the cookies. Store the treats in a fridge for up to 7 days.

Chapter 4 – It's What's on the Inside that Matters: Filling Recipes for Whoopie Pies

Cinnamon and Cream Cheese Filling

Serving: 18 whoopie pies

Total Time: 10 minutes

Ingredient List:

- 4 ounces cream cheese, softened
- ½ teaspoon vanilla
- ½ pound powdered sugar, sifted
- ¼ teaspoon cinnamon
- ¼ cup unsalted butter, softened

Instructions:

a. Cream the butter and cream cheese until light and fluffy. Gradually beat in the powdered sugar, followed by the cinnamon, and vanilla.

Chocolate-Chip Filling

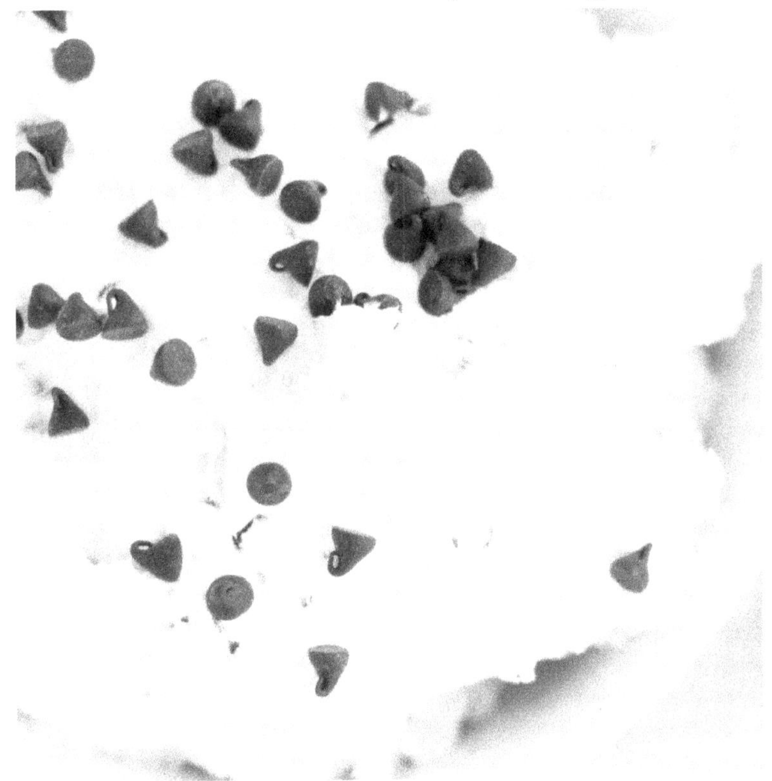

Serving: 12 whoopie pies

Total Time: 10 minutes

Ingredient List:

- ½ cup brown sugar, packed
- 8 ounces cream cheese, softened

- 1 teaspoon vanilla

- 1/8 teaspoon salt

- ¾ cup mini chocolate chips

- ½ cup unsalted butter, softened

- ½ cup powdered sugar

Instructions:

a. Blend the cream cheese and butter until fluffy. Mix in the brown sugar, vanilla, powdered sugar, and salt. Fold in the chocolate chips.

Marshmallow Buttercream

Serving: 16 whoopie pies

Total Time: 10 minutes

Ingredient List:

- 7 ounces marshmallow cream

- 1 ¼ cups powdered sugar, sifted

- ¾ cup unsalted butter, softened
- 2 teaspoons vanilla

Instructions:

a. Cream the butter until smooth and fluffy. Gradually beat in the sugar until well mixed.

b. Whisk in the vanilla, followed by the marshmallow cream and continue to mix for several minutes until well combined.

Irish Cream Filling

Serving: 9 to 16 whoopie pies

Total Time: 10 minutes

Ingredient List:

- Heavy cream
- 1/3 cup shortening
- ½ cup unsalted butter, softened
- 1 tablespoon flour, all-purpose
- 1 teaspoon Irish Whiskey
- 1/3 cup Irish Cream
- 1 ¼ cups powdered sugar, sifted

Instructions:

a. Cream the butter, sugar, and shortening together until well combined. Mix in the flour, and Irish whiskey until well incorporated.

b. Pour 1/3 cup of Irish cream into a measure cup. Add just enough heavy cream to bring the total liquid measurement to ½ cup.

c. Add the mixture from Step 2 into the mixture from Step 1, and blend until smooth and fluffy.

Cream Cheese Filling

Serving: 12

Total Time: 10 minutes

Ingredient List:

- 6 ounces cream cheese, softened
- ¼ cup unsalted butter, softened
- ½ teaspoon vanilla
- 1 ½ cups powdered sugar, sifted

Instructions:

a. Beat the cream cheese until smooth.

b. Cream in the butter, followed by the powdered sugar and vanilla. Continue to beat until the icing is smooth and creamy.

Vanilla Bean Filling

Serving: 12 to 20 whoopie pies

Total Time: 10 minutes

Ingredient List:

- 1 teaspoon vanilla
- 2 ½ cups whole milk
- 1 vanilla bean
- 1 cup unsalted butter, softened
- 2 tablespoons heavy cream
- 3 cups powdered sugar

Instructions:

a. Whip the butter until smooth.

b. Scrape the seeds out of the vanilla bean and into the butter. Cream until fluffy.

c. Whip in the milk, heavy cream, vanilla extract, and powdered sugar until well combined. The filling should be light and fluffy.

Chocolate Fudgy Filling

Serving: 10 to 12 whoopie pies

Total Time: 10 minutes

Ingredient List:

- 2 ½ cups powdered sugar, sifted
- 2 ½ tablespoons milk
- ½ cup unsalted butter, softened
- ½ cup cocoa, unsweetened
- ½ teaspoon vanilla

Instructions:

a. Combine the butter and powdered sugar together until smooth. Add in the vanilla, cocoa, and milk until fully incorporated.

b. Use the filling immediately or chill in the fridge until ready.

Lemon Filling

Serving: 16 whoopie pies

Total Time: 10 minutes

Ingredient List:

- 1 lemon, juiced and zested
- 8 ounces cream cheese, softened
- 4 cups powdered sugar, sifted
- 5 tablespoons unsalted butter, softened

Instructions:

a. Cream the butter and cream cheese together until smooth, light, and fluffy. Add the 1 tablespoon of fresh lemon juice and mix. Fold in the zest from one lemon.

b. Gradually mix in the powdered sugar until fully incorporated. Use immediately.

www.ingramcontent.com/pod-product-compliance
Lightning Source LLC
Chambersburg PA
CBHW072037150726
47999CB00002B/954